ONE CHINA POLICY

CORNEL GENERAL

Copyright © Cornel General
All Rights Reserved.

Contents

CHAPTER I

Introduction

One China is a political position according to which there is a single nation-state in the world under the name "China" and that therefore mainland China, Hong Kong, Macau and Taiwan are all part of that single national entity called "China".

This principle is actively upheld by the government of the People's Republic of China and determines that, for the Beijing regime, the island of Taiwan has the *de facto* rank of a simple "rebel province" which can never be recognized as an independent state. Acceptance or rejection of this principle is a key factor in relations between the People's Republic of China, which governs mainland China, Hong Kong, and Macau, and the Republic of China, which governs the island of Taiwan, and the surrounding islands of Pescadores, Quemoy, Matsu, Pratas, and Taiping.

The "One China" policy is strictly supported by the People's Republic of China, which equates *China* with the PR China and maintains that the only existing China has the Beijing regime as its legitimate government. In application of this principle, the PR China requires all countries with whom it maintains diplomatic relations to recognize the Beijing regime as the sole government of China and therefore refuse to maintain diplomatic relations with Taiwan, considering Taiwan also as "part of the PR China". Recognition that there is only one China (although not limited to the CHINESE PR in the definition) is also a prerequisite the PR China has put in for negotiations with the government of the Republic of China.

The position of the <u>Republic of China</u> towards this policy is appreciably more divided. Legally speaking, the Republic of China continues to maintain its own version of the "One China" principle, officially holding that the <u>Taipei</u> regime is the only "legitimate government" in all of <u>mainland China</u>. However, these claims are no longer actively held by the Taiwanese government.

The parties of <u>*Taiwan's pan-blue Coalition*</u> accept the *One China* policy, but they do not equate "China" with the <u>People's Republic of China</u> but with Taiwan itself, denying all legitimacy to the PR China regime, when one of its leaders, former <u>Kuomintang</u> (KMT) Party Chairman <u>Ma Ying-jeou</u>, went further by declaring in 2006 that "*One China is the <u>Republic of China</u>*".

In contrast, Taiwan's <u>*pan-green Coalition*</u> parties reject the *One China* position, preferring to regard Taiwan as a "separate and different" nation-state from China. They propose that the Taipei regime abandon its claims to mainland China and declare Taiwan an independent state, with no political ties to PR China. This position is also rejected outright by the government of the PR China.

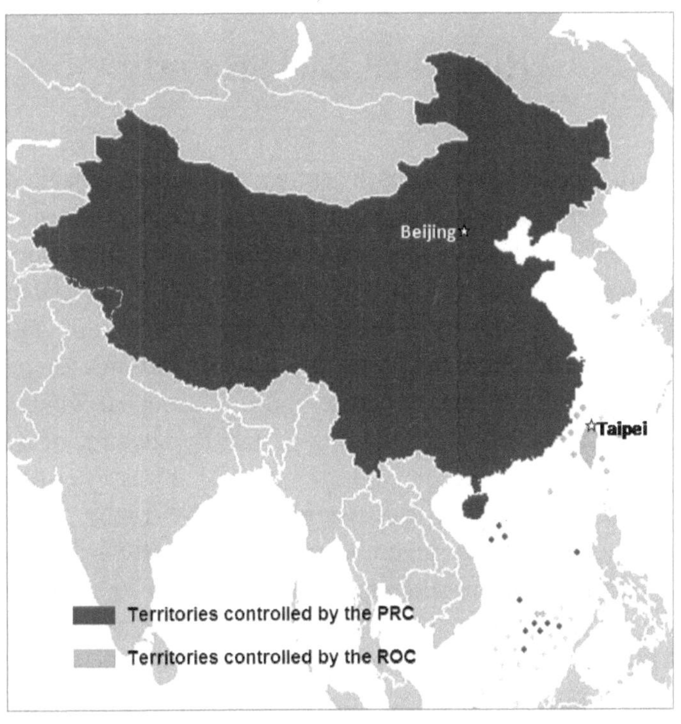

Beijing
Taipei
Territories controlled by the PRC
Territories controlled by the ROC

CHAPTER II

Historical Background

Before the early seventeenth century, Taiwan was inhabited mainly by Taiwanese aborigines, but demographics began to change with successive waves of Han Chinese migration. Taiwan was first placed under the control of the Dutch (1624-1662), the main drivers of Han immigration, and the Spanish (1626-1642, only in northern Taiwan). Zheng Chenggong (Koxinga), a Ming loyalist, occupied Taiwan in 1662 as the Kingdom of Tungning, before being incorporated by the Qing Dynasty in 1683. It was also ruled by the Japanese for half a century (1895-1945), while France briefly dominated northern Taiwan in 1884-1885.

It was a peripheral prefecture of Fujian Province under the Qing Manchu government of China from 1683 until 1887, when it officially became a separate province from Fujian-Taiwan. Taiwan remained a province for eight years until it was ceded to Japan under the Treaty of Shimonoseki in 1895.

While Taiwan remained under Japanese control, the Qing Dynasty was overthrown and the First and Second Republics of China (ROC) were established from the Beiyang regime to the Kuomintang (KMT) beginning in 1928.

After the Japanese surrender ceremonies of October 1945 in Taipei, the capital of Taiwan Province, Taiwan once again became China's system of government during the period of military occupation. In 1949, after losing control of most of mainland China after the Chinese Civil War, and before the post-war peace treaties came into force, the government of the Republic of China under the KMT withdrew to occupied Taiwan. Chiang Kai-shek declared martial law. It has been argued that Japan formally renounced all of Taiwan's territorial rights in 1952 in the San Francisco Peace Treaty, but neither that treaty nor the peace treaty signed between Japan and China granted Taiwan's territorial sovereignty to the Republic of China. The treaties left Taiwan's status, as ruled by the Republic of China or the People's Republic of China, deliberately vague, and the question of legitimate sovereignty over China is the reason Why China was not included in the San Francisco Peace Treaty.This argument is not accepted by those who consider that Taiwan's sovereignty has been legitimately returned to the Republic of China at the end of the war.Some argue that the Republic of China is a government-in-exile, while others maintain that it is a residual state.

The government of the Republic of China still rules Taiwan, but it was transformed into a free and democratic state in the 1990s after decades of martial law.During this period, Taiwan's legal and political status has become more controversial, with more public expressions of Taiwan's feelings of independence, which were previously banned.

CHAPTER III

Views within Taiwan

Within Taiwan, there is a distinction between the positions of the Kuomintang (KMT) and the Democratic Progressive Party (DPP).

The Kuomintang upholds the "one-China principle" and holds that, according to the Constitution of the Republic of China (approved by the Kuomintang government in 1947 in Nanjing), the Republic of China has sovereignty over most of China, including, according to its interpretation, both mainland China and Taiwan. After the Communist Party of China expelled the Republic of China in the Chinese Civil War from most of Chinese territory in 1949 and founded the People's Republic of China, the Chinese Nationalist government of the Republic of China, which still controlled Taiwan, continued to claim legitimacy as the government of all China. Under former President Lee Teng-hui, additional articles were added to the constitution of the Republic of China in 1991 so that it would effectively apply only to the Taiwan area.The Kuomintang proclaims a modified form of the "One China" principle known as the "1992 Consensus." Under this "consensus," both governments "agree" that there is a single sovereign state encompassing both mainland China and Taiwan, but disagree on which of the two governments is the legitimate government of this state. Former President of the Republic of ChinaMa Ying-jeou had reaffirmed his claims to mainland China until October 8, 2008.

The Democratic Progressive Party does not agree with the "One China principle" as defined by the KMT. Instead, he has a different interpretation and believes that "China" refers only to the People's Republic of China and states that Taiwan and China are two separate countries, therefore there is one country on each side and "one China, one Taiwan". The DPP's position is that the people of Taiwan have the right to self-determination without outside coercion.Current President Tsai Ing-wen refuses to affirm the 1992 consensus.

The one China principle of the People's Republic of China faces opposition from supporters of the Taiwan independence movement, which pushes to establish the "Republic of Taiwan" and cultivate a separate identity apart from China called "Taiwanization."

CHAPTER IV

An Introduction to People's Republic of China (PRC)

The People's Republic of China (PRC) is a country in East Asia. It is the world's most populous country with a population of more than 1.4 billion people. China spans five geographical time zones and borders 14 countries, the second most of any country in the world after Russia. Covering an area of approximately 9.6 million square kilometers (3,700,000 sq mi), it is the world's third largest country. The country consists of 23 provinces, five autonomous regions, four municipalities and two Special Administrative Regions (Hong Kong and Macau). The national capital is Beijing and the most populous city and financial center is Shanghai.

Modern Chinese trace their origins to a cradle of civilization in the fertile basin of the Yellow River in the North China Plain. The semi-legendary Xia dynasty in the 21st century BCE and the well-attested Shang and Zhou dynasties developed a bureaucratic political system to serve hereditary monarchies or dynasties. Chinese writing, Chinese classic literature and the Hundred Schools of Thought emerged during this period and influenced China and its neighbors for centuries to come. In the third century BCE, Qin's wars of unification created the first Chinese empire, the short-lived Qin dynasty. The Qin was followed by the more stable Han dynasty (206 BCE – 220 CE), which established a model for nearly two millennia in which the Chinese empire was one of the world's foremost economic powers. The empire expanded, fractured and re-unified was conquered and reestablished, absorbed foreign religions and ideas and made world-leading scientific advances such as the Four Great Inventions: gunpowder, paper, the compass and printing. After centuries of disunion following the fall of the Han, the Sui (581–618) and Tang (618–907) dynasties achieved what the Roman Empire could not: reunification of the empire. The multi-ethnic Tang welcomed foreign trade and culture that came over the Silk Road and adapted Buddhism to Chinese needs. The early modern Song dynasty (960–1279) became increasingly urban and commercial. The civilian scholar-official or literati used the examination system and the doctrines of Neo-Confucianism to replace the military aristocrats of earlier dynasties. The Mongol invasion established the Yuan dynasty in 1279, but the Ming dynasty (1368–1644) re-established Han Chinese control. The Manchu-led Qing dynasty nearly doubled the empire's territory and established a multi-ethnic state that was the basis of the modern Chinese nation, but suffered heavy losses to foreign imperialism in the 19th century.

The Chinese monarchy collapsed in 1912 with the Xinhai Revolution, when the Republic of China (ROC) replaced the Qing dynasty. Japan invaded China in 1937, starting the Second Sino-Japanese War and temporarily halting the civil war between the Chinese Communist Party (CCP) and the Kuomintang (KMT). The surrender and expulsion of Japanese forces from China in 1945 left a power vacuum in the country, which led to renewed fighting between the CCP and the Kuomintang. The civil war ended in 1949 with the division of Chinese territory: the CCP established the People's Republic of China on the mainland while the Kuomintang-led ROC government retreated to the island of Taiwan. Both claim to be the sole legitimate government of China, although the United Nations has recognized the PRC as the sole representation since 1971. From 1959 to 1961, the PRC implemented an economic and social campaign called the Great Leap Forward that resulted in an estimated 15 to 55 million deaths, mostly through starvation. China conducted a series of economic reforms since 1978 and entered into the World Trade Organization in 2001.

China is currently governed as a unitary one-party socialist republic by the CCP. China is a permanent member of the United Nations Security Council and a founding member of several multilateral and regional cooperation organizations such as the Asian Infrastructure Investment Bank, the Silk Road Fund, the New Development Bank, the Shanghai Cooperation Organisation and the RCEP. It is also a member of the BRICS, the G8+5, the G20, the APEC and the East Asia Summit. It ranks among the lowest in international measurements of civil liberties, government transparency, freedom of the press, freedom of religion and ethnic minorities. The Chinese authorities have been criticized by political dissidents and human rights activists for widespread human rights abuses including political repression, mass censorship, mass surveillance of their citizens and violent suppression of protests.

China is the world's largest economy by GDP at purchasing power parity, the second-largest economy by nominal GDP and the second-wealthiest country. The country is one of the fastest growing major economies and is the world's largest manufacturer and exporter. China is a recognized nuclear-weapon state with the world's largest standing army by military personnel and second-largest defense budget. China is considered to be a potential superpower due to its large markets, growing military strength, economic potential and influence in international affairs.

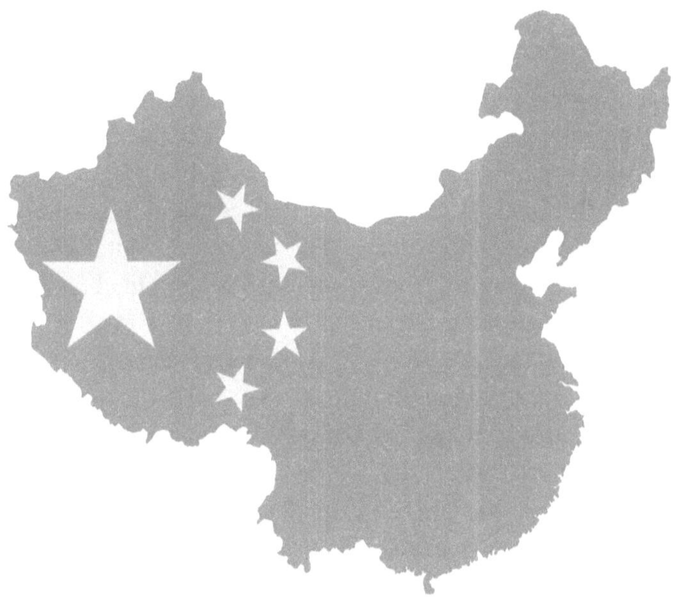

Map of the People's Republic of China (PRC)

CHAPTER V

An Introduction to Republic of China (ROC)

The Republic of China (ROC) is a country in East Asia at the junction of the East and South China Seas in the northwestern Pacific Ocean with the People's Republic of China (PRC) to the northwest, Japan to the northeast and the Philippines to the south. The territories controlled by the ROC consist of 168 islands with a combined area of 36,193 square kilometres (13,974 sq mi). The main island of Taiwan, formerly known as Formosa has an area of 35,808 square kilometres (13,826 sq mi) with mountain ranges dominating the eastern two-thirds and plains in the western third, where its highly urbanised population is concentrated. Taipei, the capital forms along with New Taipei City and Keelung the largest metropolitan area of Taiwan. Other major cities include Kaohsiung, Taichung, Tainan and Taoyuan. With around 23.9 million inhabitants, Taiwan is among the most densely populated countries in the world.

Taiwan has been settled for at least 25,000 years. Ancestors of Taiwanese indigenous peoples settled the island around 6,000 years ago. In the 17th century, large-scale Han Chinese immigration to western Taiwan began under a Dutch colony and continued under the Kingdom of Tungning. The island was annexed in 1683 by the Qing dynasty of China and ceded to the Empire of Japan in 1895. The Republic of China, which had overthrown the Qing in 1911, took control of Taiwan on behalf of the Allies of

World War II following the surrender of Japan in 1945. The resumption of the Chinese Civil War resulted in the ROC's loss of mainland China to forces of the Chinese Communist Party (CCP) and consequent retreat to Taiwan in 1949. Its effective jurisdiction has since been limited to Taiwan and smaller islands.

In the early 1960s, Taiwan entered a period of rapid economic growth and industrialisation called the "Taiwan Miracle". In the late 1980s and early 1990s, the ROC transitioned from a one-party military dictatorship to a multi-party democracy with a semi-presidential system. Taiwan's export-oriented industrial economy is the 21st-largest in the world by nominal GDP and 19th-largest by PPP measures, with a focus on steel, machinery, electronics and chemicals manufacturing. Taiwan is a developed country ranking 20th on GDP per capita. It is ranked highly in terms of civil liberties, healthcare and human development.

The political status of Taiwan is contentious. The ROC no longer represents China as a member of the United Nations after UN members voted in 1971 to recognize the PRC instead. The ROC maintained its claim of being the sole legitimate representative of China and its territory, although this has been downplayed since its democratization in the 1990s. Taiwan is claimed by the PRC, which refuses diplomatic relations with countries that recognise the ROC. Taiwan maintains official diplomatic relations with 13 out of 193 UN member states and the Holy See, though many others maintain unofficial diplomatic ties through representative offices and institutions that function as de facto embassies and consulates. International organisations in which the PRC participates either refuse to grant membership to Taiwan or allow it to participate only on a non-state basis under various names. Domestically, the major political contention is between parties favouring eventual Chinese unification and promoting a pan-Chinese identity, contrasted with those aspiring to formal international recognition and promoting a Taiwanese identity into the 21st century, both sides have moderated their positions to broaden their appeal.

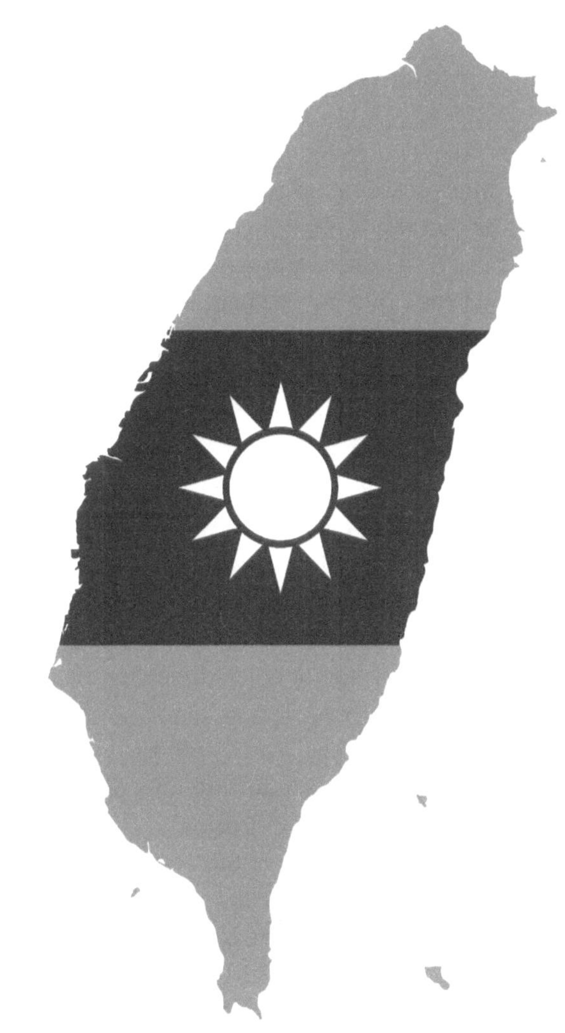

Map of the Republic of China (ROC)

CHAPTER VI

Policy Developments

One interpretation, which was adopted during the Cold War, is that the People's Republicof China or the Republic of China is the only legitimate government in all of China and that the other government is illegitimate. While much of the Western bloc maintained relations with the Republic of China until the 1970s under this policy, much of the Eastern bloc maintained relations with the People's Republic of China. While the government of the Republic of China considered itself the remaining obstacle to the legitimate rule of a country invaded by what it considered communist rebels, the People's Republic of China claimed to have succeeded the Republic of China in the Chinese Civil War. Although the Republic of China no longer presents itself as the only legitimate government of China, the position of the People's Republic of China remained unchanged until the early 2000s, when the People's Republic of China began to soften its position on this issue to promote Chinese reunification.

The revised position of the People's Republic of China was made clear in the 2005 Anti-Secession Law, which although it states that there is a China whose sovereignty is indivisible, does not explicitly identify this China with the People's Republic of China. Almost all laws of the People's Republic of China have a suffix "of the People's Republic of China" (prefix in Chinese grammar) in their official names, but the Anti-Secession Law is an exception. Beijing has made no major statements after 2004 identifying a China with the People's Republic of China and has slightly changed its definition of a China to encompass a concept called the '1992 Consensus': both sides of the Taiwan Strait recognize that there is only one China: both continents China and Taiwan belong to the same China, but they agree to differ on the definition of which China.

One interpretation of a China is that there is only one geographical region of China, which was divided between two Chinese governments during the Chinese Civil War. This is largely the position of current supporters of Chinese reunification in mainland China, who believe that "one China" should eventually be reunited under one government. Since 2005, this position has come close enough to the position of the People's Republic of China, allowing for a high-level dialogue between the Communist Party of China and the Pan-Blue Coalition of the Republic of China.